Turn Your Mortgage Into A Pension

Library and Archives Canada Cataloguing in Publication

Johnson, Gordon P., 1954-, author
      Turn your mortgage into a pension / Gordon P. Johnson
; Cynthia Assen.

ISBN 978-1-77141-069-4 (pbk.)

1. Mortgages--Canada. 2. Pensions--Canada. 3. Finance, Personal--
Canada. I. Assen, Cynthia, 1991-, illustrator II. Title.

HG5159.J63 2014   332.63'2440971   C2014-904227-2

Turn Your Mortgage Into A Pension

Gordon P. Johnson

First Published in Canada 2014 by Influence Publishing

Book Cover Design: Marla Thompson
Illustrator: Cynthia Assen
Typeset: Greg Salisbury
Photographer: Lauren Johnson

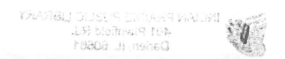

I dedicate this book with deepest love and gratitude to my best friend and wife Janice. Her unfailing encouragement and support during our life together have been a tremendous source of strength, joy, passion, and profound contentment. I am truly blessed to have her and my two daughters, Lauren and Alise, and Alise's husband, Brett, in my life.

An inscription on a church in Sussex, England, purported to have been written in 1670 reads as follows:

A task without a vision is drudgery;
A vision without a task is but a mere dream;
A vision with a task is the hope of the world.

"A must-read for anyone with a mortgage or plans to retire. It questions our traditional views and lays the foundation for all of us to improve our finances."
Bryan Dar Santos, Editor-in-chief, Life Cents Magazine

"'Turn Your Mortgage Into a Pension' is a much-needed book. An accessible and enjoyable guide for the "financially challenged" and the "financially well-versed" alike, it offers timely advice that, combined with proper financial planning, can set out a clear path towards reaching your retirement goals."
Marcin Drozdz, Director & Board Member, NEMA (National Exempt Market Association)

"Johnson's book presents important financial strategies and tools that the majority of people haven't heard about until now. Comprehensive, insightful and potentially life-changing, 'Turn Your Mortgage Into a Pension' should be read by anyone trying to take charge of their financial future."
Kevin Ziolkoski, Managing Partner, Blueprint Global Partners, a leader in connecting private placement in the marketplace

Acknowledgements

I am where I am today because of people who have come into my life and choices I have made in response to circumstances in my life. I was adopted into a wonderful, loving family by parents who made life safe, adventurous, and blessed. I was taught that the best investment you could ever make was to spend time with your family. The best legacy you could ever leave was a strong faith in God. My parents modelled this calling and I am eternally grateful.

My father was an early influence in my financial services career; in the beginning, as a mentor, and later as a business partner. He didn't always understand my fascination with thinking outside the box, but gave me much encouragement to do so.

My wife, Janice, has been my greatest source of joy and love throughout our 35 years together. She has taught me the true meaning of contentment, and has always encouraged me to reach for my dreams while keeping my feet on solid ground. She is the true rock in our family and my two wonderful children, Lauren and Alise, are a testament to her unwavering commitment, love, and devotion to her family. We are truly blessed to have her in our lives.

My financial journey incorporated many diverse and interesting paths which ultimately led me to where I am today. In my earlier days, I always seemed to be a little restless—never quite satisfied with where I was or what I had. I would set higher goals for myself, both personally and professionally. Some would call that drive and a positive trait. For me it fostered discontent.

I was teaching the basics of financial planning to the brokers, and was implementing the principles in my own financial life. But I wasn't convinced that the picture of a more secure financial future displayed on the cover of the box could be achieved with these particular puzzle pieces; some pieces were missing, some were the wrong size, and others belonged to a different puzzle altogether.

I was introduced to the book *Rich Dad Poor Dad* by Robert Kiyosaki, and the pieces started to transform themselves and fit together. One of the missing pieces in the puzzle was cash flow. That book changed my life, and is a must-read for anyone interested in gaining financial literacy.

My next "ah ha" moment came during a webinar with Robin J. Elliott, the guru of joint ventures. Robin has focused on using joint venture leverage to help thousands of business owners increase their sales and profits. www.leverageadvantage.com

I started to think differently about how to use joint ventures in my own business, and as a result I focused more on developing referral partners and less on individual effort. I was privileged to meet Robin in person a couple of years ago and thank him personally for the profound influence he had in my business endeavors.

Numerous clients over the years have encouraged me to write my strategy down, not only as a reminder to them of how to implement the mortgage pension strategy, but also as a means of sharing the concept with others.

I had the very fortuitous pleasure of being introduced to Julie Salisbury, the founder and president of Influence Publishing. Without Julie and her wonderful team, this book may never have come to fruition. Their vision of what the book not only could be, but what it should be, has constantly motivated me towards its completion.

My sincere desire in sharing with you, my reader, is that *Turning Your Mortgage Into A Pension* will inspire you to take action and control over your cash flow now and in the future. I trust that I am able to supply you with the missing pieces to your own financial puzzle.

Table of Contents

Introduction

This book presents a strategy that will turn your mortgage into a pension, as I am doing with my mortgage.

The process is applicable to anyone who has or is considering getting a mortgage. Whether you are just starting employment, nearing retirement, or are even retired, you can implement this strategy. You will learn about the strategy and how it can work for you now or in the future. I have shared the strategy with people in their twenties, as well as people in their sixties. Personally, I didn't implement the strategy until I was in my fifties. Shortly after you begin turning your mortgage into a pension, you will create a modest additional cash flow. By continuing to follow the process, you will find that your cash flow will increase.

In the book, I give an example of how your income can conservatively grow to an additional $800 per month. How can you create this extra pension without any further outlay of funds? There are a few pieces to the puzzle. Let's start putting them together.

What I write about works in Canada. Please consult your legal and tax professionals if you live in another country before you consider implementing this strategy. The average person in Canada is receiving little advice on their retirement preparations, or has given up on the prospect of retiring as they had once envisioned. People are confused. There is so much conflicting advice available that the average person cannot possibly sort it all out.

And if the plan entails additional cash flow, it just isn't feasible. Does the following scenario sound familiar?

We have a meeting with our friendly life insurance agent/financial planner, who completes a needs analysis for us. Surprise! We are in need of an additional $500,000 in life insurance; we should have critical illness insurance, and, of course, we need to start putting away a few hundred dollars every month into our RRSP. The cost of this plan is only $500 per month, a small amount to ensure that our family is protected now, as well as to ensure that we will have a wonderful retirement.

Is she right? Perhaps she is.

The problem is that we don't have $500 monthly to set aside. We are stretched as it is; we don't even have $50 monthly to set aside! We may like the sound of the plan. It makes a lot of sense to us. But what we are really thinking is, "We can't commit to this! We are going backwards every month already. Our son needs braces, our daughter has a school field trip to Europe next summer, and the car needs new tires.

The job promotion I was counting on just disappeared. There is absolutely no way that we can institute that type of plan." We politely tell our financial advisor that we need more time to think it over.

I have heard many variations on this theme during my career. The sad thing is most of the insurance agents/financial planners are in the same position themselves. If the situation were reversed, they would give the same response.

There are a lot of very good financial planners in the industry. They take their work very seriously, learn everything they can to offer the best advice possible to their clients, and truly have their clients' best interests at heart. They are proud of their industry and how they are able to move their clients forward financially.

Sadly, the average Canadian does not benefit from traditional financial advice when it comes to retirement. They just don't have the cash flow to participate in any type of costly plan.

Of course, there are high wage earners who greatly benefit from financial planners and advisors, wealthy individuals who benefit from private banking, and a shrinking percentage of workers who benefit from great pension plans. I am not primarily speaking to them.

I am speaking for and to the rest of us—the majority who don't know where to turn and won't seek out a financial planner or advisor because they don't have any money to invest. They are too busy surviving financially to even consider planning for the future!

What can be done?

Read on.

Note: There is a chapter of Qs and As that should answer the majority of the questions you may have.

Financial terms that are bolded can be found in the glossary at the end of the book.

Chapter One

What If I Stopped Working Today?

Cash flow. Two words with a huge meaning. It pays the bills. Without it we are in big financial trouble. We can't live on credit forever. I well remember the day the light came on, and an amazing thought occurred to me.

I remarked to my wife, "Do you realize that if you and I both stopped working today our income goes to zero?"

She cautiously and carefully answered the obvious. "Of course I do. That is why we work."

I continued, "I mean all our income comes from working. We don't have any **passive income**. We have some investments and **RRSPs** [Registered Retirement Savings Plan funds], but they don't create cash flow."

"Well, you're the financial strategist. What are you going to do about it?" And then she walked away, leaving me with a question that made me think long and hard.

I was on my own. At the time, I was teaching financial planning the way I had been taught, but it wasn't creating any immediate cash flow.

Go to school; get a good job; pay yourself first; get a mortgage to buy a home;

pay it off; stay out of debt; invest in a diversified portfolio of equities for the long term; retire debt-free; and enjoy your retirement.

That, in a nutshell, is a simplified version of financial planning.

However, look around at the retired people you know. Are they living the retirement life they were hoping for by following this model? Or are they just getting by, adjusting their expectations to survive?

Why aren't some *retired people* better off, despite "trying to do things right"?

Go to school; get a good job; pay yourself first; get a mortgage to buy a home; pay it off; stay out of debt; and invest in a diversified portfolio of equities for the long term.

But are they retiring debt-free? Is their retirement "set"? Often retirement is not even close to what was anticipated.

So what happened? Where is the cash flow to ensure a comfortable retirement? They followed the advice given to them. Even though they have substantial **assets**—home, vehicles, mutual funds, savings, and other investments—many wouldn't say they have the cash flow that they expected.

It is important to note, however, that some retirees and early baby boomers have pension plans from the companies that employed them for most of their working careers. They also purchased homes that have skyrocketed in value, allowing them to build up substantial assets which they may also use to fund retirement incomes. In those situations, many people are actually better off in retirement than they were during their working years.

If they purchased a home in a major centre like Vancouver or Toronto during the 1970s or 1980s, and have utilized the equity in their homes, they have done very well indeed. But not all are in that situation.

Many people past the age of sixty-five are struggling with inadequate pensions and minimal equity in their homes. They may have purchased their home later in life, suffered a marriage breakdown or financial setback, or transferred to a community where home values are substantially greater than the community they left. For them, retirement is being pushed further out, and the possibility of working well past traditional retirement age is the stark reality.

Their supposedly "golden years" are looking a bit tarnished.

What about the next generation? Many pension plans have changed from **Defined Benefit Plans** to **Defined Contribution Plans**. Many companies do not offer any type of retirement plan. What if you change employers? A pension plan, if available through your previous employer, will either stop accruing, transfer to your new employer, or transfer to a personal **LIRA (Locked In Retirement Account)**.

Home prices are substantial, with little upward potential. During the past decade (2004-2014), house prices have made huge gains, in some cases doubling or even tripling in value. Is it reasonable to expect this trend to continue? It is quite probable that in the future any increase in the value of a home will be limited to the rate of inflation. This scenario would certainly affect one's expectations of using the equity in their home to fund retirement.

What chance does the current generation have to buy and pay off a home, considering the average salary and current cost of living? How can they possibly have excess funds to invest? If they do have investments, has investment performance met their expectations? Do they even understand what their investments are?

Chapter Two

Golden Goose Now, or Future Next Egg?

Why are we taught to invest for the long term—seeking growth in a diversified portfolio of **equities** (i.e. **mutual funds**)? We need growth in order for our assets to increase in value. That is logical. Why do we need our assets to increase in value? So that at retirement, this nest egg of investments will have grown into a sizeable pool of assets, which can then be utilized to create an income (cash flow). Basically, it means building a nest egg through saving and investing.

Let's see how this works.

If you invest $3,000 per year and receive a 6 percent return for thirty years, you will have approximately $250,000 in investment assets at the end. Sounds like a lot. As a matter of fact, it is more than most people will have at their retirement.

At retirement, you convert this nest egg into a monthly income. Let's say that you can earn the same 6 percent return. So $250,000 at 6 percent equals $15,000 per annum. This equates to $1,250 per month. What? That's all? Thirty years of saving and investing, and you only get $1,250 per month? And who can save for thirty years? You would have to start at age thirty-five. As if saving for a retirement that is thirty years away is a huge priority! There are far too many current expenses, and thirty years is a long time.

There is a danger in projecting values thirty years into the future. Using the earlier mentioned example, we are looking at an additional $1,250 per month income. In 2014, the maximum Canada Pension Plan retirement benefit payable at age 65 is $1,038.33 per month. An additional income of $1,250 would definitely increase a person's standard of living. What we haven't taken into account is inflation. Suffice it to say that as inflation eats away at our purchasing power, it generally also increases our income. Should the two move in unison, we are generally okay.

Our $3,000 annual investment should increase each year by the rate of inflation in order to keep the example realistic. However, to simplify the equation, I am keeping the figures constant at today's rates.

The problem is we don't have the $3,000 per year to invest for the next thirty years. What we do have is a mortgage, car loans, household living obligations, and unexpected expenses like a new roof, furnace, or medical emergency.

So there I was—a financial planner by designation (CFP), a financial strategist by vocation, earning a decent living, children in university, car payment, mortgage payment, RRSP contributions, investment loan, and all the other payments that go along with life—looking forward to a carefree, self-sufficient retirement. Exactly what would my retirement look like?

The way things were, I was struggling to put even $3,000 per year into my RRSP. Grow for thirty years! That would put me in my eighties—I had planned on retiring earlier.

That is the precise dilemma I found myself in. That was reality and my wife was looking to me to find a solution.

I was looking at a substantial reduction to our current income in our retirement. Our dreams were headed for a huge paradigm shift, unless I could figure out how to shorten the timeframe (from thirty years to twelve), increase our annual investment contribution (more than the current $3,000 annually), and hopefully end up with a larger lump sum investment (nest egg) at the end.

It doesn't take a genius to figure out what scenario was in the cards for us. I think I wore out a calculator trying to figure out a solution!

In May 2012, *Forbes*, one of the best magazines for financial advisors, published an article entitled "Wake Up! Buy and Hold Doesn't Work." The point of the article is that perhaps we have a broken system. Most of our advice comes from life insurance companies, banks, mutual fund companies, and securities companies. Collectively, *they* make billions of dollars in profits annually; yet *we* struggle to get ahead.

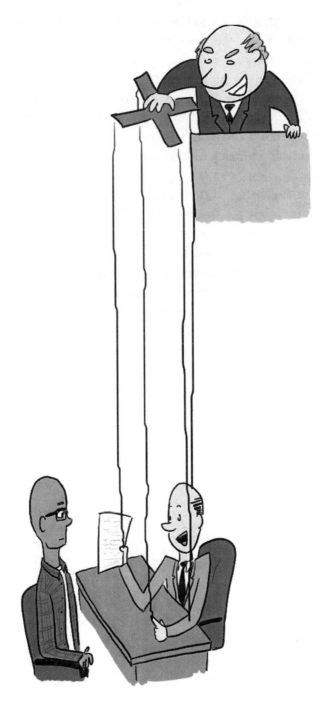

Could it be that we are led down a path that benefits the large corporations at our expense? Are we being sold products that actually serve the best interest of the corporations rather than us? Could we be paying too much for unhelpful products that enrich corporations rather than consumers? If so, then the financial planning advice we are given does not benefit us as much as it benefits the corporations who supply us with the products. They are making billions of dollars in profits while we continue to struggle.

Why are the banks and mutual fund salespeople constantly telling us to invest for the long term (retirement), building our future nest egg at the expense of current cash flow? Yet banks and mutual fund businesses thrive on cash flow themselves. Do you realize that our investing for the long term (our nest egg) actually creates cash flow for those businesses? We are advised to invest in the nest egg while they have the golden goose!

I wrote this book for those of us who are looking to create current cash flow of our own, as we wait for our investment assets to grow. For many of us, our emergency fund is a credit card. Most people could benefit from more day-to-day cash flow, even if they have RRSPs and mutual funds!

And retirement is approaching faster and faster.

Chapter Three

Open the Cash Flow Tap

What does it mean to be financially independent? The answer may vary quite widely, depending on your lifestyle, but the definition I like is as follows: a person is financially independent when their personal resources create enough passive income to cover their monthly expenses.

Quite simply, if you require $3,000 a month to live, and your passive/investment/joint venture income is $3,000 per month, you are financially independent.

There are basically four types of income: earned income, passive income, investment income, and joint venture income.

Earned income is income you get from working. When you have a job, you earn a salary or commission. **Passive income** is income that comes to you without your having to work for it. Passive income may come from a business you own that someone else runs for you. It may come from royalties from writing a song or a book. Each time the song is played on the radio or downloaded or the book is sold, you earn passive income. **Investment income** is derived from money you have invested—either in paper assets (dividend paying stocks, bonds, term deposits, mutual funds, etc.) or perhaps in real estate, which generates rental income. **Joint Venture income** is generated by facilitating a transaction between parties that benefits both parties and generates a referral fee for you. To illustrate: Person A has a network of contacts and Person B has a service or product to sell. Person C introduces the two parties and receives a referral fee for each sale generated. This may be a one-time fee or it may be ongoing. A true joint venture is a win-win-win for all parties involved: Person A, Person B, and Person C all benefit from the transaction and create income from their joint efforts.

This list is not intended to be comprehensive—just a few examples for clarification.

Earned Income

Passive Income

Investment Income

Joint Venture Income

Once I realized that I needed to understand the difference between the four types of income to truly create a pension income (passive income), I started to get excited. I now had a direction. I knew what I needed. I just had no idea how to increase my cash flow without my wife and I working additional hours or getting second jobs. The traditional investments I was using weren't creating cash flow; they were all geared toward my future nest egg. I needed to start the cash flow now, in order to transition into my dream retirement of financial independence.

I started to attend free "get rich quick" seminars. What I learned is that the presenter was getting rich quick by selling his surefire course for only a few thousand dollars! The plan was guaranteed to make me rich—only if I followed his explicit formula. I didn't buy it. Literally, I didn't buy it. I didn't spend one cent on those courses.

There is a whole industry of "experts." There is even an industry teaching you how to become an expert. Just pay a few thousand dollars and you can learn how to become an expert in a few hours and teach others to do what you do. Be a messenger and charge for your knowledge. To say the least, I was becoming more and more skeptical about this whole "think like wealthy people do and become rich" approach to life.

I started to read and re-read financial books by authors like Robert Kiyosaki and David Chilton that had been sitting around on my bookshelf for many years gathering dust. I even went out and bought a few new books. At least Robert Kiyosaki understood that cash flow is king. I started to look at things from a different perspective. I realized that nothing really had changed. The terminology had changed, the products may have changed, but the message had not. Yet the world had changed hugely.

How can we live in a world that has changed, prepare to retire into a world that will continue to change, and do so with products and a mindset that haven't changed?

What if the whole financial industry is broken and we don't even know it? Traditional financial planning may not work going forward. I started to notice a change in the way I was looking at things. Cash flow primarily comes from **fixed assets**. That is what I was being told on a regular basis. *Cash flow actually comes from many sources, but for the seminar presenters it seemed as if real estate were the main source of potential cash flow.*

Then all I needed to do was build a portfolio of real estate assets, and my retirement dream would soon be a reality. Real estate investments have many profit centres, but I am only looking at the cash flow aspect since that is my primary focus. Let's look at an arbitrary investment rental house.

Example: $1,000 monthly rent (income) minus $750 mortgage payment (expense), minus property tax, property management fee, maintenance, insurance, etc. of $175 (expense) equals net income of $75.00 monthly.

As per my example, I knew I could expect approximately $75 per month per property, net after all expenses. I arrived at this net figure by subtracting all the monthly expenses from the monthly rent.

So, to get an income of $1,250 per month would require purchasing seventeen properties ($75 x 17 = $1,275). Seventeen properties? You've got to be kidding! Where would I ever get the down payment together for seventeen properties?

This wasn't going to be as easy as I had hoped. I was still searching for the magic formula. Something had to be there. Something that just made sense. Something that I could learn and incorporate within my existing cash flow.

I didn't need a plan that called for me to put away more funds each month. I just didn't have any more funds available to put away. And I suspect that most of the people reading this book are in the same boat.

Chapter Four

Is Work the New Retirement?

Unfortunately, for most people, the first time they receive passive income instead of earned income happens at age sixty-five when they retire and **CPP (Canada Pension Plan)** and **OAS (Old Age Security)** begin. This is the first time in their lives that money actually comes to them through a source that isn't a job. And this money isn't enough. "Freedom 55" has become Freedom 85 or maybe even Freedom 95! Work is the new retirement.

That's the position I was heading toward myself. I knew a lot about the financial world and financial products, but this knowledge just wasn't working for me. I asked other advisors, in confidence, if they found themselves benefitting from their own advice. Were they taking their own advice? Were their clients benefitting from their advice? The answers I received were not surprising. "No, no, and no." Very few financial advisors believed that they would retire comfortably, and neither would their clients.

I really needed to continue looking outside the box.

I attended a financial seminar where the speaker held a senior position at a major bank. He started off by saying, "Financial planning doesn't work in Canada."

At first I thought he was making the statement to shock us—after all, most of the attendees were in the financial services industry. And then I became defensive: "Of course it works. We are all trained professionals, and we work hard at looking after our clients and their financial futures."

And then he started to recite some statistics for the average Canadian wage earner: the average debt, the average wages, the average savings, average retirement plans, etcetera. Not at all optimistic. We make an income that would have thrilled our parents, yet most of us are average—and the average person in Canada is going backwards financially.

He then went on to say, "The problem is that we don't control our cash flow."

What? Did he actually say what I thought he did? Cash flow! Now I was captivated. What was he inferring about cash flow?

He explained that until we control our cash flow we can't control our finances.

"Who controls our cash flow? The banks do. They set up numerous profit centres—mortgages, lines of credit, credit cards, chequing accounts, savings accounts, RRSPs, TFSAs [Tax Free Savings Account], mutual funds, etcetera, etcetera, etcetera—and all of them are profit centres for the banks."

How can we control our cash flow when the banks are controlling it for us to their advantage?

Most of us manage our daily finances by depositing our income into a variety of chequing accounts and savings accounts, while also borrowing through mortgages, lines of credit, loans, and credit cards. All of these are profit centres for the bank. We receive little or no interest on the money we deposit, and we pay higher interest on the money we borrow. Very efficient for the bank; very inefficient for us.

We all need banks. Some of us use banks more than others. What is a bank and how do they actually make their billions in profits year after year?

According to Wikipedia, "A **bank** is a financial institution and a financial intermediary that accepts deposits and channels those deposits into lending activities, either directly by loaning or indirectly through capital markets. A bank is the connection between customers that have capital deficits and customers with capital surpluses."

Confusing? Are we customers with capital surpluses? Do we have some money to put in the bank—either in a savings account or a term deposit? Are we customers who have capital deficits? Are we in need of money? We are buying a car or a house or the latest big-screen TV, and are short the necessary funds to make the purchase.

We are in luck! It just so happens that we don't have to go asking friends and family for a loan after all. There is a friendly institution right on the corner that is a financial intermediary (a bank). In other words, a bank is a go-between. Banks accept money from people wanting to earn interest on their deposits (savers) and lend that money out to people who need it to cover their capital deficit (spenders).

Imagine the following scenario:

"Hi, Ms. Banker, I need a $5,000 loan to buy a car."

"Why, aren't you just the luckiest person! Ms. Finance-Wise just deposited $5,000 into her savings account and we can let you have that. Let me see. Oh yes, we are giving her 1 percent interest so you can have your loan at 1 percent!"

Sound familiar? I didn't think so. The first part is very likely; the second part, not so much. Most likely the bank will charge Ms. Need-A-Loan 6 percent to 8 percent (at current rates), and will keep the **spread** (the profit margin) for themselves. Poor Ms. Finance-Wise should be happy with her 1 percent interest, as her money is safe.

What else does Ms. Finance-Wise use her bank for? She has a chequing account into which she deposits her paycheques. She makes her payments from this account, and at the end of the month the bank sends her a statement—by mail or electronically—and charges her $15 to $20 a month for the privilege of having her chequing account at their banking institution. Does she earn interest on this chequing account? Probably not. But she most likely runs a positive balance in this account for most of the month.

Let's assume that Ms. Finance-Wise deposits a total of $4,000 into her bank account each month ($2,000 each payday). In the middle of the month (the first payday), $2,000 is deposited and she now has a balance of $2,000—for a few days anyway. Over the course of the next two weeks, her account reduces to $1,000 (she pays her bills). Toward the end of the month (the second payday), another $2,000 is deposited, and her account is now $3,000. Alas, it is now the end of the month, and she has to pay the remainder of her bills, including her mortgage. Her account returns to zero. Then the process starts over again the next month.

Now the interesting part of this scenario is that for most of the month, her chequing account is in a positive position. Yet the interest earned is zero. That's right—zero. This is a *chequing* account. She pays service charges, but doesn't earn any interest. Yet, her funds are available for the bank to lend out. The bank earns interest on her funds that it loans out, yet charges her for the account.

Ms. Finance-Wise also has a $250,000 mortgage. She did her **due diligence** and found the best five-year rate available (let us assume 4.0 percent). Her mortgage is not at the same bank as her chequing account and her $5,000 **term deposit** (her emergency fund). Each month, she withdraws from her chequing account to cover the mortgage payment at her other bank.

Now let's take a snapshot of Ms. Finance-Wise's net position with her banks. She has a mortgage of $250,000; $5,000 in term deposits (earning 1 percent); and a positive bank balance of $2,000 in her chequing account. That gives a net position of minus $243,000 ($7,000 deposits and $250,000 borrowing).

The banks have created three profit centres for themselves from Ms. Finance-Wise's transactions, and they are earning interest or fees from each one of them.

1. Interest on the mortgage.
2. Interest spread between the term deposit (1 percent paid to Ms. Finance-Wise) and the interest earned on lending the funds out (4 percent mortgage to someone else).
3. Monthly bank service fees on the chequing account.

Great business model—for the bank!

Chapter Five

Your Savings and Income Should Work for YOU

There's more to Ms. Finance-Wise's story. In addition to her mortgage and bank accounts, she also has a car loan of $4,000 at 7 percent interest. All of her banking obligations (mortgage and car loan) and accounts (chequing account and term deposit) are separate. Each of these transactions is a profit centre for the bank. She has been advised to keep funds aside for a potential emergency. Recall that she has $5,000 in her term deposit, which is earning 1 percent.

It would make financial sense to pay off the car loan with $4,000 of the term deposit. However, if she does that, she no longer has an emergency fund. Having that fund gives her peace of mind, even though it continues to cost her 7 percent interest (on the funds borrowed for the car loan).

Let's look at this a little closer. What does it cost Ms. Finance-Wise to pay off her mortgage? Remember, she has a $250,000 mortgage. Let's assume her payments are $1,300 per month (4 percent interest and principal). She has **amortized** the loan (spread the payments) over twenty-five years. If everything stays the same—she consistently pays $1,300 per month for the next twenty-five years — she will be paying out a total of $390,000. That is $1,300 per month for three hundred months.

$390,000-$250,000 = $140,000

That is a whopping $140,000 in total interest! The real cost of her mortgage is $390,000!

Actually, no. It gets worse. We are missing an important part of the equation.

Since the mortgage is paid in after-tax dollars, the total amount is much higher. What does the term "after-tax dollars" mean? It means that before we receive our paycheque, the government deducts taxes. For example, let's assume that Ms. Finance-Wise is in the 20 percent effective income tax bracket. For every dollar she earns, the government takes 20 percent before her paycheque is deposited into her bank account. If she earns $2,500 gross per paycheque, then $500 will be deducted for income tax before her employer deposits her paycheque. Ms. Finance-Wise earns $5,000 monthly and pays effective tax of $1,000 monthly (20 percent), leaving her with a net monthly income of $4,000.

Let's focus on the mortgage payment using the same effective 20 percent tax rate. Ms. Finance-Wise pays $1,300 monthly for her mortgage, but must earn $1,625 (before tax) to be left with $1,300 (after-tax dollars) to make her payment.

$1,625 (earned) x 20% (effective tax rate) = $325 (income tax)

$1,625 - $325 = $1,300 (net income)

What does the actual cost of her mortgage become when we add the interest and the taxes to the principal? The answer to this question is $487,500.

$1,625 x 300 months (25 years) = $487,500

In total, Ms. Finance-Wise must earn $487,500 over twenty-five years in order to pay $1,300 per month mortgage payment through to its completion in twenty-five years.

How can this be? Her total income tax over twenty-five years (20 percent of $487,500) is $97,500. As well as this, she pays a total of $140,000 interest on her $250,000 mortgage. *Then* she has to pay the mortgage loan principal of $250,000!

Let's add the numbers for income tax, mortgage interest, and mortgage principal:

$97,500 + $140,000 + $250,000 = $487,500

How could she possibly save for retirement if her $250,000 mortgage is actually costing her $487,500? Isn't that incredible? You look after the banks ($140,000 interest) and the government ($97,500 income tax), but are struggling to look after your own retirement.

As an aside, two other factors enter into the total amount you will pay for your house: total income and your province of residence. Let's compare British Columbia and Ontario. In British Columbia, the effective tax rate on an annual income of $60,000 would be approximately 18%; in Ontario it would be approximately 19%. The difference doesn't seem like very much, but in reality Ms. Finance-Wise would have to earn an extra $20 per month to pay her mortgage if she lived in Ontario.

$20 x 12 months x 25 years = $6,000

In Ontario, the total cost of her home would be $6,000 more than if she lived in British Columbia due to the higher effective tax rate.

In British Columbia, the total cost of her home would be $487,500.

In Ontario, the total cost of her home would be $493,500.

Let's now assume that Ms. Finance-Wise earned $100,000 annual income rather than $60,000. In British Columbia, her effective tax rate would be approximately 24 percent; in Ontario, it would be 26 percent. The total cost to pay off her house in British Columbia now rises to $513,000; $527,100 in Ontario.

This may be a weak argument that it is better to earn less money! The more you make in income, the more you pay for your house. Just a passing thought, although it is a slight consolation for those earning less money than their neighbours. This may also be a benefit for the self-employed. A benefit of being self-employed may be the ability to reduce taxable income through deductible business expenses. Self-employed individuals may give up paid medical benefits, company pension plans, and group benefits, but may pay less for their houses! All this and most self-employed individuals only work half days—and, better yet, get to choose which twelve hours they want to work each day.

So, is it better to live in British Columbia than Ontario? I had better leave that argument alone!

Ms. Finance-Wise has a mortgage, a car loan, a term deposit, a savings account, and a chequing account because she has been taught to keep them separate. Each separate account is a profit centre for the bank. You've got to admit they have a brilliant business model.

We *are* putting our savings and income to work. The only problem is this money is primarily working for the bank, not for us. The bank is lending out our idle funds (savings and earnings in our chequing account) at a higher interest rate than the rate they are paying us to keep them in the bank—and keeping the spread for their profit.

When you look at a bank's financial statement, your savings are the bank's liability, and your mortgage is the bank's asset.

Which direction is cash flowing? As far as the bank is concerned, cash flows *to you* if you have savings. The interest paid to you comes out of the bank's profit. If you have a mortgage, then cash flows *to the bank* when you make your payment.

Is there a more efficient way to do our banking than having numerous separate accounts? Is there a way to increase *my* profits, rather than the bank's ?

How you bank is just as important as *where* you bank. With a non-traditional, flexible all-in-one bank account, you can consolidate various borrowing and savings accounts. An all-in-one bank account will simplify your banking and help control your cash flow. More importantly, it will set up the foundation for the strategy that will turn your mortgage into a pension.

When you open an all-in-one account, you may be able to borrow up to 80 percent of the appraised value of your home (under current mortgage rules, which do change fairly often). Think of it as a chequing account with a huge **line of credit** attached to it.

So how can the all-in-one bank account work for us? Simply by combining all our debt and savings into one account. That's it.

Let's continue with the example we've established. Ms. Finance-Wise's house is valued at $325,000. She can borrow up to 80 percent of its appraised value (subject of course to her getting qualified based on her financial picture) and transfer her debt and savings into the account. She has a $250,000 mortgage, a $4,000 car loan, a $5,000 term deposit, and savings of $2,000. She owes $247,000 (borrowings of $254,000 and savings of $7,000). She would pay one low interest rate on the net amount of $247,000. And the interest rate is **simple interest**, calculated daily, not **compounding interest** as were her previous borrowings.

What happens on payday? Under her current banking arrangement, she receives a net pay of $2,000 twice monthly. Her chequing account increases by $2,000 at each deposit, yet she doesn't receive any interest on this increased amount in her chequing account. She pays interest on her total borrowings for her mortgage and her car loan.

However, under the all-in-one bank account, the $2,000 twice monthly deposits make an immediate difference. On payday, $2,000 gets deposited and immediately the outstanding loan amount drops from $247,000 to $245,000. She only pays simple daily interest on what she owes at the time. She is paying less interest on $245,000 than when she owed $247,000. Every day that even a dollar of her savings or income stays in her account, she has less total debt and so, she pays less interest.

As she pays her bills throughout the next two weeks, the amount may rise again to $247,000. When the next $2,000 is deposited, the outstanding amount reduces again to $245,000. The savings and income deposited into an all-in-one account reduce the total interest owed—which in turn reduces outstanding debt faster. It's simple. One all-in-one account, instead of several accounts, will save you interest. That is putting your savings and income to work for you. You work hard for your money. Doesn't it only make sense to have your money work hard for you?

Suffice it to say that even though mortgage rules have changed a few times since I opened my all-in-one account, the strategy hasn't changed. In June 2012, the banks' prudential regulator, the Office of the Superintendent of Financial Institutions, introduced a new mortgage underwriting guideline for banks and other federally regulated financial institutions. This guideline outlines some key principles for prudent mortgage underwriting that banks are required to follow. It also limits homeowners to borrowing no more than 65 percent of the value of their properties through a home equity line of credit; this is down from 80 percent previously.

You can still qualify for 80 percent of the appraised value of your home, but only 65 percent of the total borrowings are now subject to simple interest, calculated daily. Fifteen percent of the total debt must now be placed into a sub-account, amortized like a traditional mortgage, and subject to compound interest (65% + 15% = 80%). This is a change from when I established my all-in-one account where the full 80 percent was calculated at a daily simple interest. For purposes of simplicity, I will explain the all-in-one banking model the way I have mine set up.

You use what you own to reduce what you owe. Brilliant!

Chapter Six

Bad Debt vs Good Debt

That's a lot of information presented on banking. Honestly, I had never given any thought to the role banking actually plays in my financial affairs. Big mistake! Huge mistake! By being ignorant, I had literally given the banks thousands of my hard-earned dollars in interest payments; this money should have been working for me! Once interest is paid to the bank, it is gone forever. It is now the bank's income, and is no longer available for *me* to invest and create cash flow for *me*!

I was depressed! Dejected! Morose. Downcast.

Here I was, teaching financial planning, and I had never even brought the equation of how to control cash flow into the very foundation of my workshops. But a glimmer of light was beginning to break through.

Yes, the financial world has changed, and perhaps so have the financial products that are now being offered. Maybe it isn't just the same old products for a different time. Perhaps the products have been there all along, or perhaps new products are indeed being introduced to the public. Maybe they just weren't offered through the traditional outlets. I just had to keep looking.

I attended another seminar. The ad in the paper promised that I would learn how to create cash flow by buying property with nothing down. "Yeah," I thought. "Nothing down except money!" You can't buy property with nothing down. You need a down payment. But the catch in the presentation was this: Don't use your money; use other people's money (**OPM**).

The facilitator went on to build a concept of joint venturing with other people. You use their money and your expertise. Of course, for a few thousand dollars, I could sign up for his full-length course which would teach me all I needed to know about how to become an expert. No thanks. Not interested.

And then he said something that caught my attention. He said, "I have a mortgage. Every wealthy person I know has a mortgage. It's the cheapest money you will ever borrow."

Why would a wealthy person have a mortgage? That didn't make any sense to me. Wouldn't a wealthy person be able to pay off their mortgage? That's what you're supposed to do—and as soon as possible. Every financial planning model that I was aware of promoted a debt-free retirement. Pay off your mortgage. That was the number one rule for financial freedom. Go into retirement debt-free. No mortgage, no credit card debt, no car loan. No debt. Nothing.

My parents went into retirement debt-free. My wife's parents went into retirement debt-free. I was hoping that I would go into retirement debt-free. Wasn't that the goal, the dream of the average person? Yet more and more, I have become aware that perhaps this is no longer a realistic expectation for most people. We look at the mortgage payment as rent. We don't believe that we will ever pay off the mortgage—certainly not at today's housing prices!

Why would wealthy people have a mortgage? They choose to. There is **bad debt** and **good debt.** What is the difference? Interest on bad debt is not tax-deductible; for example, when you borrow to go on a vacation, buy a TV, or a car for personal use, the interest you pay on the borrowed money cannot be claimed as a tax deduction. Interest on good debt, however, is tax-deductible because the money you borrow is used for the purpose of investing. In this situation, you are expected to earn income from the borrowed money. Canada's *Income Tax Act* states that any interest expense incurred to purchase investments that produce dividends and/or interest qualifies for a tax deduction. Borrow to buy a big-screen TV and the interest is not deductible. Borrow to invest in a private mortgage and the interest is tax-deductible.

Let's look at an example of good debt and bad debt. Let's say you make $25 per hour. That is called gross pay. You don't actually get the $25 per hour. You have to pay income tax, EI (employment insurance), and CPP to Canada Revenue Agency (CRA) before you receive the net income which is yours to spend. Let's assume that the total deductions come to 20 percent of your gross income. You work for $25 per hour; however, $5 of that wage goes to CRA. Your net income (spendable income) is $20.

$25 x 20% = $5

$25 - $5 = $20

The 20 percent interest rate you think you are paying on your charge card is actually much higher when you use the charge card for personal expenditures—like the big screen TV. For example, if you have a balance of $5,000 on your charge card, the annual interest at 20 percent is $1,000. But in order to pay the $1,000 in interest, you must earn $1,250 (the real rate on the charge card is 25 percent).

$5,000 x 25% = $1,250

Remember that interest is paid *after* tax is deducted from your gross income. The expenditures become prohibitively more costly should you not pay off your charge card in full every month.

On the other hand, if the interest is tax-deductible, the interest becomes a tax deduction. If interest is tax-deductible, then you can deduct the amount from your annual income *before* income tax is calculated. In other words, if you borrow funds to invest, and the total annual interest is $1,000, you deduct that $1,000 from your total income before paying income tax. To be clear, you are not borrowing on the credit card to invest! You are borrowing from your all-in-one account.

If you earn $40,000 annually, and subtract $1,000 *before* income tax is paid on the $40,000, it means that your taxes are now calculated on $39,000. This is a positive scenario. You pay less tax on $39,000 than you do on $40,000.

Conversely, if you pay income tax on the $40,000 *first* and pay $1,000 *afterwards*, you will have initially paid more in tax.

Back to our interest example: $1,000 in annual interest—if tax-deductible—saves you 20 percent in taxes or $200.

$1,000 x 20% = $200

To recap: If the $1,000 interest is bad debt (not tax-deductible), you must earn $1,250 to pay it. If it is good debt (tax-deductible), then you would save $200 in taxes.

So why would the wealthy have a mortgage? They most likely

have paid down their mortgage and then re-mortgaged to invest the funds. As the purpose of these funds is now for investment—not for the house—the interest is tax deductible. This is referred to as good debt.

This concept didn't come to me out of the dark. I had been aware for some time of the concept of leveraging to invest. I was also quite familiar with a concept called "**The Smith Manoeuvre.**" In a nutshell, the concept lays out a strategy of how to make your mortgage tax-deductible. I liked the strategy, but the products used to implement it wouldn't work for my purposes—that is, to turn my mortgage into a pension.

The Smith Manoeuvre strategy recommends that you use a combination of a traditional mortgage and a line of credit. As you pay down your mortgage, you increase your line of credit. Then you borrow from the line of credit to invest in mutual funds. For further information on The Smith Manoeuvre, refer to www.smithman.net.

The concept is that a portion of the annual growth on the mutual funds is withdrawn to cover the interest payments on the investment loan. This is called a Systematic Withdrawal Plan or SWP. I recommend caution with this plan, as the value of investment funds (mutual funds) sometimes fluctuates widely. If the first few years produce lower-than-expected returns, there is a risk that the program will collapse, and you will end up worse off than before you implemented The Smith Manoeuvre. This strategy does not turn my mortgage into a pension. I am looking for cash flow.

Chapter Seven

Is It the Mortgage or the Mortgage Payment That Bothers You?

I came to the realization that if I could tap into the equity I have in my house (the difference between the market value of my house and the amount owed on the mortgage) and use the additional borrowed funds (from the equity in my house) to create cash flow, then perhaps it would be beneficial to keep my mortgage. This was a paradigm shift from my previous way of thinking.

Just then my wife walked into the office. I turned to her and said, "I don't think we need to be concerned about paying off the mortgage."

"Why not? We don't want to have a mortgage when we retire!"

"Is it the mortgage, or the mortgage *payment*, that bothers you?" I continued, "If we had a mortgage, but someone else made the payment, and also paid us another $1,000 per month, would you be okay with that?"

She responded positively, "Of course I would! How do we do that?"

I knew what I wanted to accomplish. I wanted to turn my mortgage into a pension, and I was determined to learn how to do that.

The all-in-one mortgage account would be the foundation of the whole strategy. *It would allow me to borrow back the principal paid down on my mortgage so that I could then invest the money to create cash flow.*

Let me explain. The traditional mortgage has a set payment consisting of principal and interest blended together into a monthly payment. As the principal is paid back to the bank, we create more equity in our property. If the market value of my house is $325,000 and the mortgage is $250,000, my equity in the house is $75,000.

$325,000 - $250,000 = $75,000

When we pay our monthly mortgage, a portion of the payment is interest and a portion is principal. When we pay back $5,000 (the principal portion of many months of blended mortgage payments) on the $250,000 principal, we now owe the bank $245,000. It is important to note that the mortgage *payment* doesn't change; it is still $1,300. However, you *will* pay less interest on the borrowed money as the principal is being paid down. That means that each month, as you make a mortgage payment, more of it will be going toward paying the principal, and less toward the interest.

Equity is a number on paper—good for net worth—but it isn't available money. We can't pay bills with equity; we pay bills with cash flow.

Our mortgage is the bank's asset. The bank wants the highest return possible on the money lent (i.e. the mortgage), so they charge **compounding interest** (interest on the principal plus interest on the interest). This is how a traditional mortgage is structured. This benefits the bank.

Our mortgage is our liability. We want to pay lower interest, so **simple interest** benefits us. An all-in-one mortgage account charges simple interest on the money borrowed (mortgage).

That is one major difference between a traditional and an all-in-one mortgage.

Let's say we find a great investment for $5,000 and go to our friendly traditional banker. "Ms. Banker, I would like $5,000 back from the principal that I have paid down on my mortgage. I have found a great investment and want to borrow money to invest, so please increase my mortgage back up to $250,000, so that I can invest the $5,000."

Not so fast. The terms of the mortgage do not allow for the funds to be given back to you. Instead, the banker may suggest that you set up a line of credit. What you need to do is pay for a current house appraisal to ensure that your house has not dropped in value, and the line of credit can be set up. That's a lot of cost involved for a $5,000 loan.

The banker might also suggest you see their in-house financial planner who might recommend that the $5,000 investment loan be placed into one of their best selling mutual funds. How would that increase my cash flow? My mortgage payment doesn't change, and I would have an additional loan payment for the investment.

NO, THANKS.

The all-in-one mortgage account works differently. When I reduce my principal by $5,000, I now have $245,000 left on my $250,000 outstanding mortgage. However, as I am only paying simple interest on the balance, my mortgage payment actually drops. (A traditional mortgage payment stays the same, even when you pay it down. Refer to the discussion on this that's just above.)

Simple interest payment on my $250,000 mortgage at 3.5 percent interest would be approximately $729 per month. Simple interest on my $245,000 mortgage at 3.5 percent would be approximately $714 monthly. That is a reduction of $15 per month for each $5,000 paid.

The all-in-one mortgage account allows me to re-borrow any principal funds that I have paid down. I have access to the $5,000 I have paid on my mortgage principal. I can write a cheque for $5,000—no need for an additional line of credit or investment loan from the bank.

As I am investing these funds, I will want to keep track of the interest I am paying on the $5,000 that I borrowed back. Why? The interest I am paying on the $5,000 is tax deductible (good debt), and I need to know the interest amount in order to claim it when tax time rolls around.

The all-in-one account allows me to set up a sub-account to track the interest on the $5,000 investment (good debt—tax deductible), separate from the main mortgage interest (bad debt—not tax deductible). The sub-account simplifies the accounting by keeping track of the interest for me. I like it simple.

Chapter Eight

I Wish I Could Be a Bank

I took another look at the pieces of the puzzle that I already had in place and started to sort out the extra pieces that didn't quite fit.

I have real estate (my home), and I have some funds to invest. After one year with the new all-in-one account, I was able to pay down my mortgage by $15,000. (Note that the previous year I paid down $8,000 with my traditional mortgage and car loan.) How was it possible to pay down $7,000 more? This is how: I combined my compound interest mort-

gage, my compound interest car loan, and my compound interest investment loan together into my simple interest all-in-one bank account. Refer to the end of Chapter Five for an explanation of how money flowing through the all-in-one account reduces total interest paid. The simple interest on the combined three loans, plus the effect of money flowing through the account (from depositing my paycheques) resulted in additional debt reduction of $7,000.

Perhaps I should look to investing the funds into real estate. I'll take out funds from *my* real estate and put them right back into another piece of real estate. That made sense to me.

Although I liked the concept of investing in real estate, I chose to look for an investment that would not require a large cash output (maximum $15,000) nor would require any property management on my part.

I attended a seminar on real estate investing, which really piqued my interest. The investment was in apartment buildings. The structure of the investment predicted a cash flow of approximately 6.0 percent annually. Upon sale or re-financing of the property (in approximately five years), the principal and any resultant capital gains would be returned to the investor. Overall, the investment was expected to return 8 percent to 10 percent annually to the investor over the time period that the investment was held.

Upon further research, I discovered that investment real estate may not create consistent monthly cash flow. Some factors that influence net rental income are as follows: unexpected maintenance expenses to the property, higher management fees, unforeseen weather damage, increased insurance costs, poor economics in the area, a lower rate of occupancy, increased utility costs, increased property taxes, etcetera. Any increase in expenses will result in a decrease in net rental income. Major expenses such as a roof replacement or a boiler replacement may actually affect net income for a number of months.

This potential lack of consistent cash flow was troubling to me. Would this type of investment be a fit for my strategy of turning my mortgage into a pension? Most likely not.

A critical point of the strategy for turning my mortgage into a pension is that *the investment itself needs to generate income to pay the interest on the investment loan, eventually pay interest on the whole mortgage, and then start to pay me a pension (money above the cost of the interest on the mortgage).* If the investment doesn't create consistent cash flow, then the investment can't consistently pay the interest on my loan.

Other than mutual funds and real estate, what else is out there? The very nature of this strategy—creating a pension—requires that I be conservative. I don't want to play the stock market, I don't want huge potential gains that may entail risk; I want to protect my principal and sustain a reasonable return.

What I really need to do is be like a bank! They make huge profits with little risk. They use other people's money to invest and keep the spread. What a brilliant concept! If only I could do the same as a bank! Why not? Why can't I do the same as a bank?

Chapter Nine

I Can Be a Bank! Or at Least Do What They Do!

What does a bank do? They take money from savers and lend it out to borrowers at a higher rate of interest than the savers receive—and keep the difference for themselves. Most bank loans are mortgages. The largest asset base for a bank is its mortgage portfolio. Do banks make billions in profits? Are the investments (mortgages) considered safe? Do the investments (mortgages) create cash flow? In each case, the answer is yes.

So can I just do what a bank does? There would be no fancy investments that I don't fully understand; no risky investments where my money is at risk; no complicated investments with fancy jargon that sounds impressive but really isn't; no investments that fluctuate up and down with the market; no investments that fluctuate depending on the price of gold or wheat or oranges. Just mortgages: simple, safe mortgages. Something I understand. We know how a mortgage works. We borrow money from a bank and make a payment every month.

The bank is the investor—they invest in my mortgage. In a sense, the bank is investing in me. I realized I had not actually thought of that before. The security is my house and my earning ability. If my credit rating shows that I have a history of paying back my loans, I am considered a good risk. The bank likes people who pay back their loans. To minimize its risk, the bank gets an appraisal to ascertain the market value of the house/property to be mortgaged, and only gives a loan up to a specified percentage of the appraised value.

For instance, Ms. Finance-Wise has a house worth $325,000. The bank will lend up to 80 percent of the value of the house ($260,000) if Ms. Finance-Wise has a good credit rating and her income justifies the mortgage payment; a bank may lend in excess of 80 percent in some circumstances.

When Ms. Finance-Wise pays back the principal, the bank needs to lend the returned money to someone else; otherwise, the funds sit idle and won't generate interest. Furthermore, the bank has to pay interest to the saver. Who is really paying the investor his return? The bank? No. It is the person who is paying the mortgage. The interest on the mortgage payment pays interest to the saver.

What a brilliant business model. We are investors (savers) when we put our money in the bank and earn interest. The bank also is an investor when it lends out mortgages to make a higher interest than is paid to the saver (investor). I want to invest like the bank. What a great idea! Even better, I want to *be* the bank and invest using other people's money to make money.

Is it possible to invest in higher interest-paying mortgages than those mortgages offered by the bank? Is it safe to do so?

Fortunately, I already knew the answer to that question. I already had this piece to the puzzle. I just hadn't been looking at the whole picture. When I realized that I needed to think like a bank, I immediately completed the puzzle with pieces that I already had at my disposal.

What is this mortgage investment model? It is a Mortgage

Investment Corporation, commonly referred to as a MIC. I had been introduced to MICs a few years ago, and was impressed with the business model.

MICs were created to make mortgage investing easy for the average person. The MIC creates a vehicle for individuals to pool their money with other investors—similar to a mutual fund. The MIC invests these pooled funds into a diversified portfolio of residential and commercial mortgages. A management company performs the day-to-day administration of the fund.

A MIC operates similarly to a bank: it collects money from savers (investors); lends money to borrowers (mortgages); collects mortgage payments (administration); pays operating expenses (including management fees to the administrators of the MIC);

and passes on net earnings (interest) to investors. One hundred percent of the net income is paid out to the investors/shareholders. Oh, wait! That *is* different from a bank. The bank keeps the interest spread whereas the MIC pays to the saver (investor) the full interest earned net of expenses.

A MIC typically lends its money out to borrowers at higher interest rates than the traditional banks do. Why can a MIC charge a higher interest rate than a bank? Why wouldn't a borrower just go to a bank and get the mortgage at a lower rate? Which borrowers might need to get private mortgages?

1. People who are self-employed—banks are not as likely to lend to self-employed individuals as private mortgage entities are. One advantage to being self-employed is the ability to write off business-related expenses against income. This will reduce net income resulting in less income tax being paid. This is a wonderful advantage when it comes to tax time, but not so much when approaching a bank for a mortgage. The self-employed are the largest group of borrowers from MICs.

2. People who desire short-term mortgages—banks like longer term mortgages (generally over one year). MICs may lend for mortgages as short as three months, six months, or up to one year—in some cases, even longer; however, those would be the exception.

3. New immigrants—with low or no credit rating or minimal income. Banks cannot lend to people without a credit rating.

4. People who need to borrow money quickly— banks may take a few weeks to fund a mortgage, even if the individual qualifies for bank financing. MICs can underwrite very quickly and sometimes speed is of the essence.

5. Developers—may require short-term building funds until the conventional banks step in with construction draws. When a contractor builds a house, he will receive draws (funds) from the bank at certain stages of completion. For example:

The contractor may require financing at each stage for his expenses before billing the bank for the draw.

Draw	Construction Stage	Approx. %	Date
1st	Gravel driveway, permits, site survey	15	30-Jan
2nd	Completion of foundation & sub-floor	20	28-Feb
3rd	Lock-up stage (framing, roofing, windows, & doors)	20	30-Mar
4th	Rough-in plumbing & electrical, furnace & duct, basement hydronic, concrete floor, drywall, rough in fireplaces, interior stone work	20	30-Apr
5th	Installation of kitchen, vanities, custom cabinets, custom stairs, flooring, trim, plumbing fixtures, garage floor	15	30-May
6th	Exterior siding, trim, stone work, concrete verandah & steps, rear concrete patio, garage driveway approach, Final completion and approval from building inspector	10	15-Jul
Total		**100**	

What I really like about MICs is that the investment return varies with the prevailing interest rate. What that means to me as an investor is that I don't have to worry if interest rates fluctuate. Remember that I am looking for a spread on my investment—just like a bank. If I have money invested in a MIC, and the prevailing mortgage interest rate increases (at the bank), the MIC will follow suit and raise their interest rates as well. The increase on mortgage rates will pass on to me as an investor.

I am thinking like a bank. As I pay down the mortgage on my home, I can borrow the money back and invest in mortgages just like the bank. If rates decrease, I expect my investment rate will decrease. If rates increase, I expect my investment rate to increase. As long as there is a spread of at least 3 percent between the borrowing rate and investment return, then I am indeed turning my mortgage into a pension.

If I borrow at 4 percent and earn 7 percent, then I am not paying the interest on those borrowed funds—the investment is! I am receiving an additional 3 percent spread from the investment! The question is: Can I consistently earn a 3 percent spread?

The following is a table I have created based on the fourteen-year returns of a MIC that I am well acquainted with. This MIC is one of the oldest and largest MICs in Western Canada. Juxtaposed is the fourteen-year base rate of the all-in-one bank account that I use for my mortgage.

What I find particularly interesting is the correlation between the two fluctuating rates. For the most part, they mirror each other. That is what is required to ensure that the strategy of turning my mortgage into a pension works in the long term. Over the fourteen-year period, the average spread is 3.86 percent.

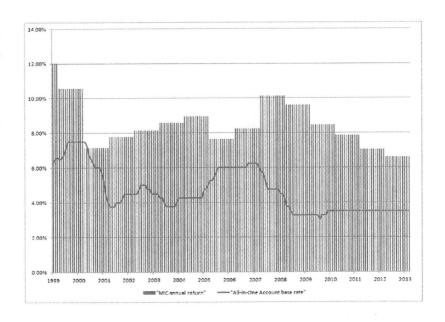

As with all investments, past results should not be used to project future results. All investments carry a certain degree of risk. I encourage anyone who wishes to explore a MIC as an investment vehicle to employ their own due diligence.

Chapter Ten

Looking into the Cash Flow Crystal Ball

How would my strategy work? I plugged Ms. Finance-Wise's information into the all-in-one bank's online calculator and came up with the following:

Traditional Mortgage

Year	Principal	Interest	Ending Balance
1	$9,215.41	$9,984.59	$244,784.59
2	$6,591.96	$9,584.35	$238,192.63
3	$6,263.80	$9,336.20	$231,928.83
4	$6,516.87	$9,083.13	$225,411.96
5	$6,780.16	$8,819.84	$218,631.80
6	$7,054.08	$8,545.92	$211,577.72
7	$7,339.04	$8,260.96	$204,238.68
8	$7,635.56	$7,964.44	$196,603.12
9	$7,944.02	$7,655.98	$188,659.10
10	$8,264.96	$7,335.04	$180,394.14
11	$8,598.87	$7,001.13	$171,795.27
12	$8,946.24	$6,653.76	$162,849.03
13	$9,307.70	$6,292.30	$153,541.33
14	$9,683.73	$5,916.27	$143,857.60
15	$10,074.95	$5,525.05	$133,782.65
16	$10,481.97	$5,118.03	$123,300.68
17	$10,905.45	$4,694.55	$112,395.23
18	$11,346.01	$4,253.99	$101,049.22
19	$11,804.41	$3,795.59	$89,244.81
20	$12,281.31	$3,318.69	$76,963.50
21	$12,777.45	$2,822.55	$64,186.05
22	$13,293.66	$2,306.34	$50,892.39
23	$13,830.77	$1,769.23	$37,061.62
24	$14,389.51	$1,210.49	$22,672.11
25	$14,970.84	$629.16	$7,701.27
26	$7,701.27	$89.28	$0.00
Total	$254,000.00	$147,966.86	

All-in-one Mortgage

Year	Principal	Interest	Ending Balance
1	$15,573.55	$8,426.45	$234,094.45
2	$16,120.01	$7,879.99	$218,142.44
3	$16,685.88	$7,314.12	$201,624.55
4	$17,271.83	$6,728.17	$184,520.72
5	$17,878.60	$6,121.40	$166,810.12
6	$18,506.94	$5,493.06	$148,471.18
7	$19,157.54	$4,842.46	$129,481.63
8	$19,831.27	$4,168.73	$109,818.35
9	$20,528.91	$3,471.09	$89,457.44
10	$21,251.35	$2,748.65	$68,374.09
11	$21,999.43	$2,000.57	$46,542.65
12	$22,774.08	$1,225.92	$23,936.57
13	$17,622.65	$461.97	$6,425.92
14	$3,152.65	$187.67	$3,273.27
15	$3,273.27	$67.06	$0.00
Total	$251,627.96	$61,137.31	

Comparing traditional mortgage rate at 4% with all-in-one rate at 3.5% on main account and 3.79% on sub-account.

Current way of paying off debt on mortgage and car: Annual debt reduction: $9,215 (from online calculator).

All-in-one account way of paying off debt: Annual debt reduction: $15,500 (from online calculator).

The above table is for illustrative purposes only and in no way implies any guaranteed future results. There are a number of assumptions provided in the data plugged into the online calculator, and it is based on current interest rates. These rates may change without prior notice. Expenses will also vary over time, ultimately affecting the rate at which the mortgage is paid down.

That being said, the result is very significant. Ms. Finance-Wise can pay off her mortgage years earlier. Ten years earlier to be exact (from online calculator). If this were her goal, the all-in-one account would certainly be a smart way to go. She would potentially save $86,800 in interest and be debt-free in fifteen years.

However, Ms. Finance-Wise also wants to turn her mortgage into a pension. With the knowledge at her disposal, she is well on her way.

At the end of the first year, she has paid down her mortgage by approximately $15,000. Her total borrowings have been reduced by $15,000; therefore, her interest payment on the borrowings has also decreased accordingly. Interest on an all-in-one account is simple interest calculated daily (as opposed to interest compounding semi-annually) and charged at the end of the month. At the current rate of 3.5 percent, her monthly interest payment has dropped by $43.75.

$15,000 x 3.5% = $525 annually (or $43.75 monthly)

Now she can borrow back the $15,000 paid down on her mortgage principal and invest the funds in a cash flowing investment like a MIC. She will set up a sub-account to track the interest on these funds, as the interest is tax-deductible. This is an important step when it comes to tax time!

This method of paying down and borrowing back to invest will create a pension plan for Ms. Finance-Wise *without her having to invest any additional funds.* That's right! She can keep her existing standard of living.

When Ms. Finance-Wise re-borrows the $15,000, the interest payment on her mortgage will increase by $43.75 per month (at the current rate of 3.5 percent), which will decrease her cash flow (less spendable monthly income). However, as the purpose of this strategy is to *increase* cash flow (more spendable monthly income), she must invest the funds where cash flow is paid to her on a consistent basis.

This is where the MIC comes in. Over the past fourteen years, the MIC that is illustrated in the preceding table has paid on average 3.86 percent more than the prevailing interest rate charged on her bank mortgage (a spread of 3.86 percent). For example, when she invests her $15,000 in the MIC, assume the investment income paid to her is 7.36 percent (3.5% + 3.86% = 7.36%). She then pays the interest on the borrowed funds from the all-in-one bank account (mortgage) currently at 3.5 percent leaving her with a profit of 3.86 percent (spread), or $48.25 monthly.

To summarize:

- $15,000 invested at 7.36 percent equals $1,104 annually (or $92 monthly).
- Interest on the $15,000 borrowed at 3.5 percent equals $525 annually (or $43.75 monthly).
- Earn $1,104; pay interest of $525.
- $1,104 - $525 = $579
- Profit is $579 annually (or $48.25 monthly).

Ms. Finance-Wise is turning her mortgage into a pension. Are you aware of any other pension plans that will pay without you contributing to the plan?

What happens the next year? A repeat of the previous year, sort of like the movie Groundhog Day, the scenario repeats itself. In the above table, the all-in-one side shows $15,000 principal paid down in the first year. When we borrow the funds back we return to the first line in the example. The principal is paid down another $15,500. Borrow back $15,000 this time and invest the funds. There is now $30,000 invested. What do these numbers look like?

- $30,000 invested at 7.36 percent equals $2,208 annually (or $184 monthly).
- Interest on the $30,000 borrowed at 3.5 percent equals $1,050 annually (or $87.50 monthly).
- Earn $2,208; pay interest of $1,050.
- $2,208 - $1,050 = $1,158
- Profit is $1,158 annually (or $96.50 monthly).

The pension is increasing.

At what point is the monthly mortgage payment paid by the investment? For this example, let's use total income from the investment and total payment of interest on the borrowed mortgage funds. I use the minimum monthly interest payment required on my mortgage as the monthly payment. When my cash flow meets the minimum monthly payment, then I consider the mortgage payment as paid by the investment.

At current rates, Ms. Finance-Wise pays approximately $730 per month minimum interest on her $250,000 mortgage. (Based on the structure I have on my mortgage for simplicity $250,000 mortgage at 3.5 percent = $8,750 annually or $730 monthly). How much investment capital is needed to generate $730 monthly?

Each $15,000 investment at 7.36 percent will generate $1,104 annual income, or $92 monthly income. She will need $8,750 annual income, or $730 monthly income to pay the minimum interest on her mortgage.

Year 1	$15,000 (total $15,000)	= $92/mo.
Year 2	$15,000 (total $30,000)	= $184/mo.
Year 3	$15,000 (total $45,000)	= $276/mo.
Year 4	$15,000 (total $60,000)	= $368/mo.

Year 5 $15,000 (total $75,000)   = $460/mo.
Year 6 $15,000 (total $90,000)   = $552/mo.
Year 7 $15,000 (total $105,000) = $664/mo.
Year 8 $15,000 (total $120,000) = $736/mo.

It will take her eight years of investing $15,000 to create $8,832 annual income, or $736 monthly income—the amount required to pay her mortgage payment.

$15,000 x 8 years = $120,000, the amount of investment capital Ms. Finance-Wise requires to pay her monthly mortgage payment.

Eight years! That is how long it potentially will take until Ms. Finance-Wise won't have a mortgage payment.

Think of it! By repeating the process of paying down her mortgage principal by $15,000 and re-borrowing to invest, in eight years, she won't have a *mortgage payment*. She will have a *mortgage*; she won't have a mortgage *payment*. That is a very important distinction. The investment is making the payment for her.

Contrast this with a traditional twenty-five-year mortgage. After eight years, Ms. Finance-Wise would still have a monthly payment of $1,300—and seventeen more years of monthly payments before she is mortgage-free.

What will be the scenario in seventeen years with an all-in-one mortgage assuming interest rates stay at current levels? The mortgage of $250,000 will be paid down to zero. Ms. Finance-Wise will have been re-investing an additional $15,000 per year in the MIC for seventeen years. That means she will have invested $255,000.

$15,000 x 17 = $255,000

At 7.36 percent, $255,000 will generate $18,768 annually ($1,564 per month). Interest on the $255,000 investment loan is $8,925 annually ($743.75 per month). Cash flow is $820 per month.

$255,000 x 7.36% = $18,768 (or $1,564 monthly)
$255,000 x 3.5% = $8,925 (or $743.75 monthly)
$1,564 - $743.75 = $820.25

Can you believe it? A pension of $820 per month after seventeen years! And it didn't require any additional financial sacrifices on Ms. Finance-Wise's part.

Contrast this with a traditional twenty-five-year mortgage again. After seventeen years, Ms. Finance-Wise would still have a monthly payment of $1,300—and eight more years of mortgage payments before she is mortgage debt-free. By switching to an all-in-one account, after seventeen years she would potentially have positive cash flow of $820 monthly instead of a mortgage payment of $1,300 monthly. That is a cash flow difference of $2,120 per month for the next eight years!

$1,300 + $820 = $2,120

That is how you turn a mortgage into a pension plan.

Let's compare. Her existing conventional mortgage will be paid off in twenty-five years. No cash flow for twenty-five years; only cash outlay. Or by implementing this strategy of turning your mortgage into a pension, cash flow increases almost immediately and continues to grow simply by adhering to the plan. How exciting is that?

It will take learning, commitment, and responsibility. Albert Einstein is credited with saying: "We can't solve problems by using the same kind of thinking we used when we created them."

I have shown you *how* (learning) to turn your mortgage into a pension. It will take commitment on your part. You will be tempted to interrupt your strategy and spend your new found cash flow on diversions that will not lead to having the MIC pay your mortgage payment, which will eventually lead to creating a pension for yourself.

Lack of self-control is self-indulgent. This is true in all areas of our life, including our finances. Don't give in.

Finally, you will have to take responsibility to make the decision to change your financial future. However, you will not be alone as you implement this strategy. There is a team waiting to work with you.

I encourage you to take action and make positive steps to retain control of your own cash flow and retirement funding. The strategy must be properly implemented in order to comply with Canada Revenue Agency's rulings.

If this book was given to you by your financial advisor, then work with him or her to properly implement this pension strategy.

Should you require help or would like to know specifically which financial products I use for my own strategy, please contact me at gordjohnson@outlook.com. I would be pleased to share my knowledge with you as you turn your mortgage into a pension.

Answers To Questions
You Didn't Know You Had

You most likely have a number of questions.
Let's look at a few of them:

Q: Are MICs the only investment that will work in this strategy?
A: Not at all, I simply wanted to describe the strategy using a very conservative model. The company used in my illustration has never lost one cent of investors' capital, and has never missed a payment to the investors.

Q: Are there other MICs that have the same or better track records than the one referred to in your example?
A: Absolutely. Again, I wanted to be conservative to demonstrate how the strategy works. Another mortgage fund I am familiar with targets an annual return of 7 percent or more to its investors, and has achieved this target return since the 2009 fiscal year.
   12.75% in 2009;
   12.21% in 2010;
   11.65% in 2011;
   9.50% in 2012; and
   8.07% in 2013

Q: What other investments are available? MICs sound great, but I want something a little more exciting.
A: Be careful. Pensions aren't too exciting, so perhaps your pension investments shouldn't be too exciting either. A lot of early baby boomers have put off their retirement plans, as their investments are not where they expected them to be at this point in their lives

Personally, I want to think like a bank, act like a bank, be a bank, while "Turning My Mortgage Into A Pension." Slow and steady. Safe and secure. Reliable and predictable.

There are a number of other investments that may work with this strategy. I prefer any investment I use to have a minimum ten-year reliable track record.

Let's look at two other potential investments.

The first one is **Syndicated Mortgages**. I am aware of a few different companies offering syndicated mortgages that have been around for at least ten years. Two that I am quite familiar with have returned on average 12 percent annually during the past ten years.

The structure for these companies is similar. The first company pays annualized returns of 8 percent (paid quarterly) with a potential bonus of 4 percent per year paid at the exit of the investment. This may equal 12 percent annualized over the term of the investment. Terms are from two to five years depending upon the project.

The second company pays annualized returns of 10 percent (paid quarterly) with a bonus of 2 percent per year paid at project completion. Terms range from two to four years depending on the project. This also equals 12 percent over the term of the investment.

Investments in syndicated mortgages are specific to a single project, which may increase the investment risk. As you will be investing with the project developer, you must do your due diligence on the developer as well as on the project.

The second alternative investment is **Leasing**. You are most likely familiar with automobile leases, but are you aware that most equipment can be leased? The leasing industry is growing at an annual rate of 20 percent, and a wide range of equipment including computers, medical equipment, dental equipment, construction equipment, office furniture, etcetera are available through leasing.

The leasing company that I am familiar with has been offering a 12 percent return to investors since its inception in 1991.

Q: What are Syndicated Mortgages?
A: A syndicated mortgage occurs when several investors collectively fund one specific mortgage. A syndicated mortgage is **collateral** registered in your personal name—security with title. Each investor has the total amount of their principal investment duly registered in their name at the Provincial Land Registry Office. This unique feature of syndicated mortgages is not available through any other product.

This type of investment was formerly available only to large investors or financial institutions. Recent changes to market conditions and mortgage legislation allow broader participation in this lucrative area of project financing.

Q: Why don't the investment advisors and bankers tell us about these alternative investments?
A: These investments are not typically recommended by the banks or by most financial advisors as they are not licensed to sell them. In Canada, investment and financial advisors must be licensed by a regulatory body in order to recommend investment products to their clients. Different products may require additional licences. For example, an advisor holding a life insurance licence can recommend and sell **segregated** funds but not mutual funds. To sell mutual funds, they must hold a mutual fund licence in addition to their life insurance licence. Should they wish to recommend and sell exempt market products, they would need to be licensed as an exempt market representative.

Exempt market investments are distributed through **Exempt Market Dealers** and **Exempt Market Representatives,** who are registered with the Provincial Securities Regulators. These investments are distributed by way of an **Offering Memorandum**.

The exempt market in Canada provides a unique opportunity to obtain exposure to transactions that were once available exclusively to **accredited investors** and **institutional investors.** Recently the investments have become more widely available to the general public with smaller minimum investments.

Q: Is this a small market?
A: Not at all. As a matter of fact the market is huge. Think in terms of **private market** versus **public market**. The exempt market is private and the mutual funds market is public. A recent disclosure that I have heard for annual investments is $140 billion for private versus $75 billion for public.

Q: What is the difference between private and public investments?
A: Typically, public markets are liquid (a *ready* market for shares— mutual funds or stock market dealers), whereas private markets are illiquid (i.e. there is no ready market for disposing of the shares). Recent private offerings in the exempt market provide the ability for investors to redeem their investment—or a portion thereof—before the term is complete.

Q: I have a 10 percent down payment. Can I use this mortgage pension strategy?
A: In order to set up an all-in-one mortgage on your property you will require a 20 percent down payment. That is the government's rule, not the bank's. You may wish to go ahead and purchase the house utilizing a traditional mortgage. Once you reach 20 percent equity—either through additional savings, mortgage pay down, or increase in the value of the property (or a combination of all three)—you can apply to replace your traditional mortgage with an all-in-one mortgage. Then you can begin to turn your mortgage into a pension.

Q: How will rising interest rates affect this strategy of turning my mortgage into a pension?
A: There are two parts to this question. The first part is that the outstanding mortgage principal will not be paid down as quickly if interest rates rise. For example: a $250,000 mortgage at 3.5 percent equals an $8,750 annual payment or $729.17 monthly. A $250,000 mortgage at 4.5 percent equals an $11,250 annual payment or $939.50 monthly. This 1 percent rise in interest

rates means that over the year you will pay down $2,500 less on your principal and will therefore have $2,500 less available to re-borrow and place into cash-flowing investments. This will stretch out the timeline for your strategy—but only slightly.

The investment portion of your mortgage should maintain the required spread as per the table shown in Chapter Nine.

Q: Can I change my mortgage before the term is up?
A: Absolutely. You will most likely have to pay a three-month penalty, and in some cases an **interest differential**.

In most cases, it does make sense to switch to the all-in-one mortgage account, even with the penalty incurred on moving your mortgage. Often the penalty to switch mortgages can be made up in a few months, as the all-in-one account is more ef-ficient with daily simple interest and reduced interest payments. This is due to cash flowing through the account (see Chapter Five).

Q: Isn't the income I receive on these investments taxed? Wouldn't that reduce the viability of this strategy? Reduce the spread?
A: Yes. The income is taxed. Remember I mentioned that any money borrowed to invest should be put in a sub-account and the interest tracked separately. This is important as the tax-deductible interest is claimed against the taxable income. Tax is paid on the difference.

Let's look at this more closely. $10,000 invested. Interest earned 7.36 percent or $736—taxable. Interest paid on the borrowed funds 3.5 percent or $350—tax-deductible. The difference is 3.86 percent or $386; that is the net amount taxable.

$10,000 x 7.36% = $736
$10,000 x 3.5% = $350
$736 - $350 = $386

Taxes will, however, reduce the net earnings and reduce the net spread depending on your tax bracket. For example, if you are in a 20 percent tax bracket, then you will pay $77.20 tax on the

$386, leaving a net amount of $308.80. The net return after tax is 3.09 percent.

$386 x 20% = $77.20

$386 - $77.20 = $308.80

$308.80 net income on $10,000 investment equates to a net return of 3.09%.

If you are in a 40 percent tax bracket, then you will pay $154.40 tax on the $386, leaving a net amount of $231.60. The net return after tax is 2.32 percent.

$386 x 40% = $154.40

$386 - $154.40 = $231.60

$231.60 net income on $10,000 investment equates to a net return of 2.32%.

Q: I am renting and don't have a mortgage—can this strategy work for me?
A: If you don't have a mortgage because you are renting, then how can you turn your non-existent mortgage into a pension? You can still invest in the various investments suggested in this book.

Q: My home is paid for. Can I still use this strategy?
A: Absolutely. You have a head start. You have access to your equity immediately; you don't have to pay your mortgage down first, as is generally the case. It is still wise to use the all-in-one bank account instead of a line of credit for this. Lines of credit tend to have a higher interest rate and do not allow sub-accounts to be set up to track your interest.

Now comes the interesting part. Once you have your mortgage paid off and you are debt-free, it is really hard to make the decision to put a mortgage back on the house. After all, you worked hard to pay it off; it feels nice and secure to be debt-free. Emotionally it just doesn't feel right to borrow against your debt-free home—even to invest and create an income.

Since this concept is new to you, perhaps start incrementally. Test it out first and get comfortable with the process. Set up your all-in-one bank account and invest $10,000. When you start receiving your investment return (to the amount that it covers your borrowing interest cost), and you are consistently earning cash flow above the cost of the borrowed funds, you may wish to increase the investment amount.

Q: What about **Reverse Mortgages?**
A: Most Canadians are heading toward reverse mortgages. They are lending the banks their money (deposits), letting the banks earn a spread on those funds, while slowly paying off their mortgage over the next twenty-five years. Then they retire and end up re-mortgaging their home (reverse mortgage) to access the equity in their home. That is unfortunate.

Let's compare a few of the many differences between the all-in-one account with a typical reverse mortgage:

- Costs to open: all-in-one account: nil; reverse mortgage: $2,000 to $3,000.
- Interest Rate: all-in-one account: typically 2 percent to 3 percent lower than reverse mortgages.
- Credit Limit: all-in-one account: available up to 80 percent of the appraised value of the home (typically 50 percent); reverse mortgage: 10-40 percent of the appraised value of the home.
- Amount Required to borrow: all-in-one account: nil; reverse mortgage: usually $25,000 to begin and smaller increments after initial borrowing.

Retirement may present a lot of what if's. Unexpected medical expenses, home repairs, travel opportunities, and perhaps even starting a small business venture! For those who choose to stay in their homes, access to the equity in the house may be a well-informed option, but choose wisely.

Q: I already have a pension. Should I use this strategy?
A: Absolutely and congratulations! Fewer and fewer Canadians have employment pensions. Those who do can always use another pension—you aren't restricted to only one! There was a time when retirement planning was used to enhance our employment and government pensions. Today, fewer and fewer Canadians can count on employment pensions, and must rely on personal resources to supplement government pensions.

Q: What if the value of our home doesn't increase?
A: If home prices only increase a little, stay level, or perhaps even decrease in value over the next few decades, you can still create a pension by implementing this strategy.

It doesn't matter what the future market value of your home is when you turn your mortgage into a pension.

Many have relied on the increased value of their home to help fund their retirement. If this happens, great! But even if your home doesn't increase in value, this strategy still enables you to help fund your retirement.

Q: Can I use these investments in my RRSPs or TFSAs?
A: Absolutely. All of these alternative (exempt market) investments referred to in this book are available for inclusion in your registered accounts. The consistent higher returns make them an excellent choice for RRSPs, TFSAs, or even RESPs.

Q: Isn't it better for our kids to inherit our house mortgage-free?
A: This is one of the most-asked questions. Let's make a comparison. Suppose your home is valued at $400,000. Upon the demise of the last surviving spouse, each child will receive proceeds from the sale of the house as specified in the will. To simplify, if there are two children, each will have an equal portion of $200,000.

This is *without* implementing the strategy.

Now, let's suppose you implemented the mortgage pension

strategy described in this book, and your $400,000 home has a $300,000 mortgage outstanding. The $300,000 has been invested in cash flowing investments with an average net 4 percent return to you after the mortgage interest payment.

The home is sold for $400,000, the mortgage is paid off ($300,000), and the two children receive the difference of $100,000 ($50,000 each). The $300,000 in investments are sold (turned into cash), which, added to the $100,000, now totals $400,000. Each child will receive half of the proceeds—$200,000.

Note: The *net result* is the same to your children *whether or not* you implement the strategy.

However, by continuing to utilize the mortgage pension strategy, you will receive an additional $12,000 annually in income equating to $1,000 per month in additional income.

$300,000 x 4% = $12,000 (or $1,000 per month)

Is it better to leave your home debt-free for the kids to inherit, or for you to receive an additional $1,000 per month income until your demise? *The kids will end up with the same amount of inheritance either way.*

Q: Won't CPP look after our retirement?
A: CPP is designed to replace approximately 25 percent of your working income. Combined with personal savings like RRSPs and TFSAs, your CPP should be considered a supplementary component to retirement income.

Most of us will have contributed to CPP for approximately forty-five years when we retire, yet the average monthly CPP payment in 2013 was approximately $600 with the maximum being not much more than $1,000.

Why not add additional income by turning your mortgage into a pension? And, unlike with CPP, you won't have to make any contributions to the strategy.

Q: What do I do after my mortgage is completely turned into a pension?
A: Are you asking if you can continue to invest? Absolutely.

Or why not spend the monthly cash flow? The whole purpose of creating a pension out of your mortgage is to increase your cash flow. Why not enjoy the fruits of your labour? Another option may be to invest in a TFSA. One of the dangers facing us in retirement is outliving our money. Inflation will erode the purchasing power of our money by increasing the cost of living each year. You may help prepare for this reality by building up your TFSA with the excess funds you are receiving. Any growth in the TFSA is tax-free and can accumulate until you require the funds to supplement your cash flow in the future. That may help you to retire more comfortably.

Q: When I implement this strategy, is this all the financial planning I need?
A: Absolutely not. A comprehensive financial plan is beyond the scope of this book. I am simply showing a way to turn your mortgage into a pension. This will free up cash flow, which you can then direct toward the other parts of your financial plan. This may entail mortgage life insurance, critical illness, wills, etcetera. Find a financial planner whom you can trust and meet with him or her. Every family situation is different, and each financial plan must be tailored for specific circumstances.

Q: Why don't you name the investments and the banks in this book?
A: There are a couple reasons for this. Firstly, although I am knowledgeable about these financial products, I am not licensed to advise on, recommend, or sell them. Secondly, companies change, products are re-named, and investments stop raising money for a particular offering. It would be difficult to remain current with this information.

Check out the following website for further information on exempt markets: www.exempteducation.ca.

Email me with any questions you may have at gordjohnson@ outlook.com. I would be happy to explain how to implement this strategy properly, and refer you to the appropriate licensed representatives.

Remember:

A task without a vision is drudgery [Paying a mortgage];
A vision without a task is but a mere dream [Paying off your mortgage];
A vision with a task is the hope of the world [Turning your mortgage into a pension].

Glossary

Most of these definitions are found at
Investopedia.com
www.investopedia.com/dictionary

Accredited Investor: Investors who are financially sophisticated and have a reduced need for the protection provided by certain government filings. Accredited investors include individuals, banks, insurance companies, employee benefit plans, and trusts.

In order for an individual to qualify as an accredited investor, he or she must accomplish at least one of the following:

- earn an individual income of more than $200,000 per year, or a joint income of $300,000, in each of the last two years, and expect to reasonably maintain the same level of income;
- have a net worth exceeding $1 million, either individually or jointly with his or her spouse;
- be a general partner, executive officer, director, or a related combination thereof for the issuer of a security being offered.

These accredited investors are considered to be fully functional without all the restrictions of the IIROC (Investment Industry Regulatory Organization of Canada). Accountability for securities regulation extends from the securities regulator to the minister responsible for securities regulation and, ultimately, the legislature, in each province.

An employee benefit plan or a trust can be qualified as an accredited investor, if its total assets are in excess of $5,000,000.

Amortized Loan: A loan with scheduled periodic payments of both principal and interest—usually monthly. This differs from loans with interest-only payment features, balloon payment features, and even from negatively amortizing payment features.

Appreciation: An increase in the value of an asset over time. This term can be used to refer to an increase in any type of asset such as a stock, bond, currency, or real estate. This is the opposite of depreciation, which is a decrease in the value of an asset over time.

Asset: An asset is anything of value that can be converted into cash. Examples of assets include the following:

- cash and cash equivalents: term deposits, chequing and savings accounts, money market accounts, physical cash, treasury bills (*aka* T-bills);
- real property: land and any structure that is permanently attached to it;
- investments: annuities, bonds, mutual funds, pensions, shares, gold, silver, etcetera;
- personal property: boats, collectibles, household furnishings, jewellery, vehicles, etcetera.

Bad Debt: Incurring debt to buy something that is not an asset and that you, not other people, have to pay back. Bad debt is not tax-deductible. Examples include vacation, big-screen TV, clothes.

Capital Gains: An increase in the value of a capital asset (investment or real estate) that gives it a higher worth than its purchase price. The gain is not realized until the asset is sold.

Capital Loss: A capital loss is incurred when there is a decrease in the value of a capital asset (investment or real estate) compared to its purchase price.

Cash Flow: Cash moving into or out of an account creates cash flow. The direction of cash flow determines whether cash flow is positive or negative. Cash inflow to my bank account is positive; cash outflow to someone else's bank account is negative. Positive cash flow from an investment is good as this creates passive income.

Collateral: Property or other assets that a borrower offers a lender to secure a loan. If the borrower stops making the promised loan payments, the lender can seize the collateral to recoup its losses. Because collateral offers some security to the lender in case the borrower fails to pay back the loan, loans that are secured by collateral typically have lower interest rates than unsecured loans. A lender's claim to a borrower's collateral is called a lien.

If you get a mortgage, your collateral would be your house.

Compound Interest: Compound interest can be thought of as "interest on interest," and will make a deposit (savings or investment) or loan (debt) grow at a faster rate than simple interest, which is interest calculated only on the principal amount.

A simple interest example: $10,000 invested for five years at 5 percent simple interest would pay $500 per year every year. The total of principal and interest after five years would be $12,500. You do not receive interest on the interest, only interest on the principal.

A compound interest example: $10,000 invested for five years at 5 percent compound interest would pay $500 the first year. The second year would pay $525 as the interest is based on $10,500. The total of principal and interest after five years would be $12,762.81. You are receiving interest on the interest, as well as interest on the principal.

For debt, the same principle applies. Simple interest is charged on the loan principal only. Compound interest is charged on the loan principal as well as on the accumulated interest on the loan. With investments, compound interest works for you. With borrowings, compound interest works against you.

CPP (Canada Pension Plan): One of three levels of Canada's retirement income system, which is responsible for paying retirement and disability benefits. The Canada Pension Plan was established in 1966 to provide a basic benefits package for retirees and disabled contributors. When the recipient dies, survivors receive the plan's provided benefits.

The CPP pays a monthly amount, which is designed to replace about 25 percent of the contributor's earnings on which initial contributions were based, and is indexed to the Consumer Price Index.

Defined Benefit Plan: An employer-sponsored retirement plan where employee benefits are sorted out based on a formula using factors such as salary history and duration of employment. Investment risk and portfolio management are entirely under the control of the company. There are also restrictions on when and how you can withdraw these funds without penalties.

Defined Contribution Plan: A retirement plan in which a certain amount or percentage of money is set aside each year by a company for the benefit of the employee. There are restrictions as to when and how you can withdraw these funds without penalties. There is no way to know how much the plan will ultimately give the employee upon retiring. The amount contributed is fixed, but the benefit is not.

Due Diligence: An investigation or audit of a potential investment. Due diligence serves to confirm all material facts with regards to a sale. Generally, due diligence refers to the care a reasonable person should take before entering into an agreement or a transaction with another party. Due diligence is a way of preventing unnecessary harm to either party involved in a transaction.

Equities: In terms of investment strategies, equity (individual stocks) is one of the principal asset classes. A stock represents ownership in a company.

Equity: In general, you can think of equity as ownership in any asset after all debts associated with that asset are paid off. In the context of real estate, equity is the difference between the current market value of the property and the amount the owner still owes on the mortgage. It is the amount that the owner would receive after selling a property and paying off the mortgage. Stocks are equity because they represent ownership in a company.

Exempt Market Dealer: An Exempt Market Dealer or EMD is a registered and qualified dealer of exempt market securities or private investments. EMDs are registered under provincial securities legislation, meaning they are required to meet compliance standards, code of conduct requirements, and proficiency standards.

EMDs ensure investments offered to clients are sound and the representatives selling them are competent professionals acting with the best interest of the clients. The EMD acts as a safety net for investors by ensuring full compliance with all regulation, both federal and provincial; employing a Chief Compliance Officer; using only licensed Dealing Representatives; and selling only those products offered by the Dealer.

Exempt Market Dealing Representative: Exempt Market Dealing Representatives register with an Exempt Market Dealer. This ensures that anyone offering exempt market products to clients have been approved for registration with the securities commission(s) in the province(s) they are conducting business; and have successfully completed either the Canadian Securities Course or the specialized Exempt Market Products exam.

Fixed Asset: A long-term tangible piece of property that a firm owns and uses in the production of its income and is not expected to be consumed or converted into cash any sooner than at the earliest one year's time. Buildings, real estate, equipment, and furniture are good examples of fixed assets.

Good Debt: Also known as leverage, using other people's money to invest by buying assets such as property or mortgages. Other people, such as tenants or mortgagees, pay the money back for you. Good debt is tax-deductible debt.

Institutional Investor: A non-bank person or organization that trades securities in large enough share quantities or dollar amounts that they qualify for preferential treatment and lower commissions. Institutional investors face fewer protective regulations, because it is assumed that they are more knowledgeable and better able to protect themselves.

Some examples of institutional investors are pension funds and life insurance companies.

Interest Differential: Fixed-rate financing has the potential for creating financial losses or the reduction of a lender's yield when capital is repaid and then lent out at lower market rates. For example, you take out a mortgage for a five-year term at 5 percent interest. The lender is counting on getting 5 percent interest for the entire term of the loan. If interest rates fall to 3.5 percent, you may want to re-mortgage to take advantage of the lower rate. Your lender will not be able to re-loan the funds at 5 percent as the new rate is 3.5 percent. To make up the loss on the interest they were expecting, they will charge a penalty equivalent to what they would have earned if you had left your loan at 5 percent for the period remaining until loan maturity.

Lease: A legal document outlining the terms under which one party agrees to rent property from another party. A lease guarantees the lessee (the renter) use of an asset and guarantees the lessor (the property owner) regular payments from the lessee for a specified number of months or years. Both the lessee and the lessor must uphold the terms of the contract for the lease to remain valid.

Liability: This term simply refers to any money or service that is currently owed to another party.

Liabilities include loans, accounts payable, mortgages, deferred revenues, and accrued expenses.

Line of Credit: An arrangement between a financial institution, usually a bank, and a customer that establishes a maximum loan balance that the bank will permit the borrower to maintain. The borrower can draw down on the line of credit at any time, as long as he or she does not exceed the maximum set out in the agreement. The advantage of a line of credit over a regular loan is that interest is not charged on the part of the line of credit that is unused, and the borrower can draw on the line of credit at any time that he or she needs to. Depending on the agreement with the financial institution, the line of credit may be classified as a demand loan, which means that any outstanding balance will have to be repaid immediately at the financial institution's request.

LIRA (Locked-In Retirement Account): A LIRA is a Canadian investment account designed specifically to hold locked-in pension funds for former plan members, former spouses, former common-law partners, surviving spouses, and surviving partners. Funds held inside LIRAs will normally only become available (or "unlocked") to holders upon retirement. The distinction between a LIRA and an RRSP is that where RRSPs can be cashed in at any time, a LIRA cannot. Instead, the investment held in the locked-in account is "locked-in" and cannot be removed until either retirement or a specified age outlined in the applicable pension legislation (though certain exceptions exist). Another important distinction between regular RRSPs and LIRAs is that once funds have been transferred from a company pension plan to a LIRA, further contributions cannot be made into said LIRA. Any monetary amounts earned in the LIRA through investment are also considered to be locked-in.

MIC: Mortgage Investment Corporations or MICs were created to make mortgage investing easy for the average investor. The MIC creates a vehicle for individuals to pool their funds, similar to a mutual fund, and invest those pooled funds into a diversified portfolio of residential and commercial mortgages. A management company performs the day-to-day administration of the fund.

Mortgage: A debt instrument (loan) secured by the collateral of specified real estate property. In a residential mortgage, a home buyer pledges his or her house to the bank as collateral for the loan. The bank has a claim on the house should the home buyer default on paying the mortgage. Mortgages are also known as "liens against property" or "claims on property."

Mutual Funds: An investment vehicle that is made up of a pool of funds collected from many investors for the purpose of investing in securities such as stocks, bonds, money market instruments, and similar assets. Mutual funds are operated by money managers. They give small investors access to professionally managed, diversified portfolios of equities, bonds, and other securities, which would be quite difficult (if not impossible) to create with a small amount of capital. Each shareholder participates proportionally in the gain or loss of the fund.

Net Worth: Your net worth is calculated by subtracting your liabilities from your assets. Essentially, your assets are everything you *own*, and your liabilities are everything you *owe*.

OAS (Old Age Security): Financed by Canadian tax dollars, OAS provides benefits to eligible citizens sixty-five years of age and older. Although there are complex rules to determine the amount of the pension payment, typically a person who has lived in Canada for forty years after turning eighteen is qualified to receive the full payment of $551.54 (current at the time this book was written) per month. OAS benefits are considered taxable income and carry certain claw back provisions for high income earners.

Offering Memorandum: A legal document stating the objectives, risks, and terms of investment involved with a private placement. This includes items such as the financial statements, management biographies, detailed description of the business, etcetera. An offering memorandum serves to provide buyers with information on the offering and to protect the sellers from the liability associated with selling unregistered securities.

OPM: Other People's Money.

Passive Income: Passive income is income that comes to you without your having to work for it. Typically investment income and some types of business income are passive.

Private Market: The sale of securities to a relatively small number of select investors as a way of raising capital. Private placement is the opposite of a public issue, in which securities are made available for sale on the open market.

The simplest definition of private equity is that it is equity that is not publicly listed or traded. Private equity actually consists of individuals and firms that invest directly into private firms. The underlying motivation for such investments is of course the pursuit of achieving a positive return on investment. Most of the private equity industry is made up of large institutional investors, such as pension funds, and large private equity firms funded by a group of accredited investors. Since the basis of private equity investment is direct investment into a firm, often to gain a significant level of influence over the firm's operations, quite a large capital outlay is required, which is why larger funds with deep pockets dominate the industry.

Private Placement: See Private Market.

Public Market: The term "public" is most commonly used to describe a company's shares or any other type of financial instrument that trades in the secondary markets. In other words, any securities that trade on an exchange and can be bought or sold by anyone in the general population are referred to as publicly traded securities.

There are thousands of companies that have shares and financial products that are available to be bought or sold by the public. These companies must file reports that meet the strict requirements of IIROC (Investment Industry Regulatory Organization of Canada). Accountability for securities regulation extends from the securities regulator to the minister responsible for securities regulation and, ultimately, the legislature, in each province.

As a result of IIROC requirements and regulations, public companies tend to be more transparent and subject to much more public scrutiny than private companies.

Reverse Mortgage: A reverse mortgage provides income that people can tap into for their retirement. The advantage of a reverse mortgage is that the borrower's credit is not relevant, and is often unchecked, because the borrower does not need to make any payments. Because the home serves as collateral, it must be sold in order to repay the mortgage when the borrower dies. In some cases, the heirs have the option of repaying the mortgage without selling the home. These types of mortgages have large origination costs relative to other types of mortgages. Senior citizen borrowers with good credit should carefully analyze the options of an all-in-one mortgage and compare them with a reverse mortgage.

RRSP (Registered Retirement Savings Plan): A legal trust registered with the Canada Revenue Agency and used to save for retirement. RRSP contributions are tax deductible and taxes are deferred until the money is withdrawn. An RRSP can contain stocks, bonds, mutual funds, GICs, contracts, and even mortgage-backed equity.

RRSPs have two main tax advantages:

- Contributors deduct contributions against their income. For example, if a contributor's tax rate is 40 percent, every $100 he or she invests in an RRSP will save that person $40 income taxes, up to his or her contribution limit.
- The growth of RRSP investments is tax-sheltered. Unlike with non-RRSP investments, returns are exempt from any capital-gains tax, dividend tax, or income tax. This means that investments under RRSPs compound tax-free within the RRSP and tax is deferred until withdrawal.

Segregated funds: A type of pooled investment that is similar to a mutual fund, but is considered an insurance product. Segregated fund proceeds received by the insurance company are used to purchase underlying assets (usually shares in companies), and then shares of the segregated funds are sold to investors. The funds are held separately from the other assets of the insurance company.

Simple Interest: Simple interest is called simple, because it ignores the effects of compounding. The interest charged is always based on the original principal, so interest on interest is not included. Not so good for investments, but good for debt.

Spread (net interest rate): The difference between the average yield a financial institution receives from loans and other interest-accruing activities, and the average rate it pays on deposits and borrowings. The net interest rate spread is a key determinant of a financial institution's profitability (or lack thereof).

In simple terms, the net interest spread is like a profit margin. The greater the spread, the more profitable the financial institution is likely to be; the lower the spread, the less profitable the institution is likely to be.

Tax-deductible: A tax deduction is a reduction on the amount of income that is subject to income tax. Such a deduction from gross income arises due to various types of expenses incurred by a taxpayer. Tax deductions are removed from taxable income (adjusted gross income) and thus they lower the overall tax-expense liability. Examples of tax deductions are union dues and RRSP contributions.

Term Deposit: A deposit held at a financial institution that has a fixed term. These are generally short-term deposits with maturities ranging anywhere from a month to a few years. When a term deposit is purchased, the lender (the customer) understands that the money can only be withdrawn after the term has ended or by giving a predetermined number of days' notice.

TFSA (Tax-Free Savings Account): An account that does not charge taxes on any contributions, interest earned, dividends, and capital gains; the funds can be withdrawn tax-free. Tax-free savings accounts were introduced in Canada in 2009 with a limit of $5,000 per year, which is indexed for subsequent years. The contributions are not tax deductible and any unused room can be carried forward. This savings account is available to individuals aged eighteen and older and can be used for any purpose.

The benefits of a TFSA come from the exemption of taxation on any income earned by assets within the investment. Withdrawals from a TFSA are also not taxed.

The Smith Manoeuvre: The Smith Manoeuvre takes advantage of the fact that while mortgage interest in Canada is not tax-deductible, interest paid on loans for investments is tax-deductible. This does not extend to loans taken for investments made in registered plans such as RRSPs and tax-free accounts, which already have their own tax breaks.

The Smith Manoeuvre was developed and popularized in a book of the same name by Fraser Smith, a former financial planner based on Vancouver Island in British Columbia, Canada. Smith calls his manoeuvre a debt-conversion strategy rather than a leveraging tactic, with its benefits including tax refunds, faster mortgage repayment, and a growing retirement portfolio.

Author Biography

After graduating from the University of British Columbia in 1976, Gordon joined his father to work in the financial services industry. Though he initially tried convincing himself that the job was not his true calling, 37 years later Gordon still loves his "job," and is passionate about financial education and creating strategies for the average person.

He earned his Chartered Financial Planner designation in 1986 (CFP) and dedicated most of his career to management and mentorship. Gordon and his father were also partners for many years at a small Managing General Agency (MGA). Gordon taught financial planning to the brokers and headed up administration of the office.

More recently, Gordon embarked on the seminar trail - teaching financial education, with an emphasis on creating and controlling cash flow. He continued searching for solutions, alternative approaches to investments, and simple strategies that could be easily understood and implemented.

Gordon's passion for financial education, stewardship, and helping people attain financial well-being has culminated in developing a strategy for turning a mortgage into a pension. He started using this strategy in his 50's, and has taught it to people from their 20's upward to their 60's.

Today, Gordon lives in Surrey, BC, with his wife of 35 years, and enjoys travelling, hiking, reading, skiing and camping.

Twitter: www.twitter.com/mortgagepension
Facebook: www.facebook.com/mortgagepension
Email: gordjohnson@outlook.com

If you want to get on the path to be a published author by
Influence Publishing please go to
www.InfluencePublishing.com

Inspiring books that influence change

More information on our other titles and how to submit your
own proposal can be found at
www.InfluencePublishing.com

CPSIA information can be obtained at www.ICGtesting.com
Printed in the USA
LVOW08s1907060914

402801LV00006B/60/P